PRACTICE SETS

JOB ORDER COSTING
AND PROCESS COSTING

TO ACCOMPANY

POLIMENI • FABOZZI • ADELBERG
COST
ACCOUNTING
THIRD EDITION

RALPH S. POLIMENI
Hofstra University

KATHLEEN VILLANI
Queensborough Community College

McGRAW-HILL, INC.

New York   St. Louis   San Francisco   Auckland   Bogotá   Caracas
Hamburg   Lisbon   London   Madrid   Mexico   Milan   Montreal   New Delhi
Paris   San Juan   São Paulo   Singapore   Sydney   Tokyo   Toronto

PRACTICE SETS: JOB ORDER COSTING AND PROCESS COSTING
TO ACCOMPANY
COST ACCOUNTING, THIRD EDITION

1 2 3 4 5 6 7 8 9 0 WHT WHT 9 0 9 8 7 6 5 4 3 2 1

ISBN 0-07-010559-6

The editor was Judy Motto;
the production supervisor was Janelle S. Travers.
The Whitlock Press, Inc., was printer and binder.

CONTENTS

Preface   iv

Job Order Costing Practice Set................................. 1

Process Costing Practice Set.................................. 45

PREFACE

This book contains two practice sets: one on job order costing and the other on process costing.

The details concerning cost accumulation have been condensed to make the sets workable yet comprehensive.

Upon completion of these two practice sets a student should have a thorough understanding of job order costing, process costing, and the accumulation of product costs.

Ralph S. Polimeni, Ph.D., C.P.A., C.C.A.
Kathleen Villani, M.B.A., C.P.A.

JOB ORDER COSTING PRACTICE SET

KELLUM MANUFACTURING CO
PRACTICE SET
JOB ORDER COST ACCOUNTING

1

JOB ORDER COSTING

INTRODUCTION

This practice set is designed to illustrate the principles and concepts of a job order cost accounting system. The student is the general accountant for a firm manufacturing electronic parts. The details concerning purchases of material, labor operations, number of completed units as well as other aspects of the accounting system have been condensed to make the set workable, yet comprehensive.

Instructions are given whenever a transaction occurs for the first time. The student will be required to enter transactions, post journal entries, make summary entries and prepare financial statements.

Upon completion of this practice set a student will have an understanding of a job order cost accounting system and the accumulation of product costs.

GENERAL INFORMATION

The Kellum Manufacturing Company, a medium size firm, uses a job order cost accounting system to accumulate product costs. The firm manufactures electronic parts and equipment to customer specifications. Materials are purchased from outside suppliers and are issued to the production and service departments.

Production begins in the machining department and the parts are then transferred to the assembly department to be finished, assembled and inspected.

The company also has two service departments. The repairs and maintenance department maintains all factory machines in efficient running condition. The utilities department furnishes the production departments with heat, water and electricity.

Service departments' costs are distributed to the production departments. The factory overhead application rate is then determined on the basis of direct labor hours and is applied when a job is completed.

Books of Account

Transactions are recorded in the following:

Journals
Cash receipts journal
Cash disbursements journal
Purchases journal
Materials requisition journal
Labor distribution journal
Sales journal
General journal

Note: The transactions for the month of January have already been recorded in the following: cash receipts journal, cash disbursements journal, and purchases journal. Summary data relating to these journals will be given at the end of the month.

Ledgers
General ledger

Subsidiary Ledgers
Work-in-process inventory (job order cost sheets)
Factory overhead (department factory overhead cost sheets)

Please note the following:

A. General ledger - Accounts are arranged in a numerical sequence (see chart of accounts). A post-closing trial balance is given which shows the beginning balances in the various accounts.

B. Work-in-process inventory ledger - Individual job order cost sheets are used to record costs of production. Spaces are provided at the top of each cost sheet for various information concerning a particular job.

    A summary section is used to arrive at total costs and estimated profit.

    The work-in-process inventory balance at January 1st, was $49,540.10.

C. Factory overhead ledger - Department factory overhead cost sheets are used as the subsidiary ledger of the factory overhead control account. Actual factory overhead is not charged directly to jobs, but to the factory overhead control account. An entry is also made on the department factory overhead cost sheet.

4

D. Only the controlling materials account will be used in this practice set. It should be understood that when the company purchases materials, the subsidiary ledger, as well as the control account, is charged with the purchase. When materials are requisitioned, the control account and the subsidiary ledger would be adjusted.

E. A weekly summary of direct and indirect labor charges is made from information gathered by the payroll clerk. The summary data is used to charged job order cost sheets with direct labor and to charge department factory overhead cost sheets with indirect labor. The labor distribution journal is also kept current to facilitate summary posting to the general ledger accounts at the end of the month.

All company employees are paid biweekly. Factory workers are paid on an hourly basis, with time and a half for overtime.

Employees are paid Wednesday for wages earned during the preceding two week period ending Saturday.

F. Factory overhead is applied based on a predetermined rate times direct labor hours. Department overhead estimates are given. The service departments are to be allocated as follows:

(1) Repairs and maintenance department is allocated to utilities and the production departments based on the number of service requests.

(2) The utilities department is allocated to the production departments based on the number of machine hours.

The factory overhead application rate is then determined on the total estimated production department factory overhead costs using direct labor hours.

The following data is used to calculate the factory overhead application rate for the machine and assembly departments.

Departments

	Machine	Assembly	Repairs & Maintenance	Util.	Total
Number of service requests	985	673	−	206	1,864
Machine hours	94,000	43,000	−	−	137,000
Direct labor hours	83,800	54,600	−	−	138,400

5

An entry is then made in the general journal and work-in-process inventory subsidiary ledger.

When a job is completed, the job order cost sheet is totalled and entered in the summary section of the cost sheet.

Costs relating to jobs still in process at the end of the month must be accrued so that a work-in-process inventory ending balance can be determined.

CHART OF ACCOUNTS

Balance Sheet Accounts (100-299)

Assets (100-199)

Current Assets (100-129)
- 101 Cash
- 103 Notes Receivable
- 106 Accounts Receivable
- 106.1 Allowance for Doubtful Accounts
- 112 Materials
- 115 Work-in-Process Inventory
- 118 Spoiled Units Inventory
- 124 Finished Good Inventory
- 129 Prepaid Expenses

Land, Plant & Equipment (130-159)
- 130 Land
- 133 Building
- 133.1 Accumulated Depreciation-Building
- 138 Factory Equipment
- 138.1 Accumulated Depreciation-Factory Equipment
- 144 Small tools
- 147 Office Equipment

Liabilities & Capital Accounts (200-279)

Current Liabilities (200-249)
- 201 Accounts Payable
- 203 Payroll Payable
- 205 Employee's Federal Income Tax Payable
- 207 FICA Tax Payable
- 210 Federal Unemployment Tax Payable
- 221 Accrued Property Tax Payable

Capital (250-279)
- 250 Capital Stock
- 262 Retained Earnings

Income Statement Accounts (300-849)

- 301 Sales
- 351 Cost of Goods Sold
- 360 Factory Overhead Applied
- 400 Factory Overhead Control
- 502 Marketing and Administrative Expenses
- 642 Interest Expense
- 704 Interest Income
- 705 Cash Discount on Purchases

Transactions for the Month of January

No. 1   Calculate the factory overhead application rate using the analysis sheet listing the estimated factory overhead costs.

January 2, Tuesday

No. 2   Issued materials costing $2,150 to job #101; Req. No. 100. When materials are issued, record the transaction in the materials requisition journal and record on the job order cost sheet. Posting to the work-in-process inventory, factory overhead control, and materials account in the general ledger will be made at the end of the month.

No. 3   Purchased small tools for $1,365. The machine department received $275, the assembly department received $180, repairs and maintenance department received $850 and utilities department $60. Enter on the department factory overhead cost sheet. No other entry is required at this time.

January 3, Wednesday

No. 4   Purchased materials for $3,100 from Specialty Supply House, terms 2/10, n/30. No entry required. Transaction included in summary data at the end of the month.

No. 5   Net wages earned as of the end of last month $56,325 are paid. Checks are issued to all employees.
Record the payment of wages in the payroll journal.
(Employees federal tax withholdings totalled $8,759.80).
Charge the payroll related expense to factory overhead control in the general journal. Also record the payroll related expenses on the department factory overhead cost sheet using the following breakdown:

FICA tax	$3,379.50
Federal unemployment tax	450.60
Total payroll related taxes	$3,830.10
Machine department	$1,761.85
Assembly department	1,110.73
Repairs and maintenance department	536.21
Utilities department	421.31
	$3,830.10

January 4, Thursday

No. 6   Charge the utilities department with $210 of supplies. Materials Req. No 101.

January 5, Friday

No. 7   Received an order from Sonic Systems, New Jersey, for 500 printed circuit boards. Job No. 126 was assigned; delivery is scheduled for March 3. A new job order cost sheet must be opened. The factory supervisor analyzes the job's materials requirements.

January 8, Monday

No. 8   Issued to Job #126 $18,500 of materials, Req. No. 102.

No. 9   The summary report of direct and indirect labor charges for the preceding week has been prepared by the payroll clerk. The report lists direct labor hours and direct labor costs for each job as well as indirect labor, overtime and supervisor's salaries.

From this report, the various jobs are charged with labor costs. The indirect labor cost, overtime costs and supervisor's salaries are also entered on the department factory overhead cost sheet. The data is then recorded in the labor distribution journal to facilitate end of the month postings.

Although jobs are charged weekly with labor costs, the payroll is paid every other Wednesday. At that time the payroll clerk will issue a report giving total wages, payroll deductions and net amount payable.

The following is the summary report for the week ending January 6. Enter the data on the job order cost sheets, department factory overhead cost sheets and the labor distribution journal.

Payroll Summary

Job. No.	Machine Department DL Hours	Machine Department DL Cost	Assembly Department DL Hours	Assembly Department DL Cost	Repairs & Maint. Dept.	Util. Dept.	Total
101	361	$1,985.50	319	$1,339.80			$ 3,325.30
105	328	1,804.00	265	1,113.00			2,917.00
108	204	1,122.00	93	390.60			1,512.60
Total direct labor		$4,911.50		$2,843.40			$ 7,754.90
Indirect labor		2,865.00		2,360.00	$2,580	$2,660	10,465.00
Overtime		480.00		375.00	–	158	1,013.00
Supervisor's salaries		5,100.00		3,200.00	1,725	900	10,925.00
Total		$13,356.50		$8,778.40	$4,305	$3,718	$30,157.90

8

January 9, Tuesday

No. 10   Received a 60 day, 9% note for $7,500 from Yan Yo Fidelity in temporary settlement of their account. Record in general journal.

No. 11   Issued 180 transistors to Job 108; cost $560, Req. No. 103.

No. 12   Issued to repairs and maintenance department $260 of supplies; Req. 104.

January 10, Wednesday

No. 13   Issued sales invoice #001 for $37,400 to Strout Industries, Illinois. Merchandise was sent air freight, terms, payable within 30 days. These goods were removed from finished goods inventory for shipment. Record in sales journal. Production costs were $28,463.

No. 14   Issued materials to Job 105, cost $2,680; Req. No. 105.

January 12, Friday

No. 15   Issued 100 special capacitators to Job 108, cost $300, Req. No. 106.

No. 16   Issued to Job No. 105 materials costing $1,800; Req. No. 107.

January 15, Monday

No. 17   The summary report of direct and indirect labor charges for the preceding week has been prepared by the payroll clerk. Enter data on job order cost sheets, department factory overhead cost sheets and the labor distribution journal.

Payroll Summary

Job. No.	Machine Department DL Hours	Machine Department DL Cost	Assembly Department DL Hours	Assembly Department DL Cost	Repairs & Maint. Dept.	Util. Dept.	Total
101	285	$ 1,567.50	188	$ 789.60			$ 2,357.10
105	291	1,600.50	241	1,012.20			2,612.70
108	410	2,255.00	266	1,117.20			3,372.20
126	299	1,644.50	136	571.20			2,215.70
Total direct labor		$ 7,067.50		$3,490.20			$10,557.70
Indirect labor		2,640.00		2,121.00	$2,285	$2,418	9,464.00
Overtime		610.00		285.00	192	–	1,087.00
Supervisor's salaries		5,100.00		3,200.00	1,725	900	10,925.00
Total		$15,417.50		$9,096.20	$4,202	$3,318	$32,033.70

9

No. 18　　　Paid Exorbitant Fuel Supply $1,800 and City Water Company $250. Charge to utilities department - factory department overhead cost sheet. No other entry is required.

No. 19　　　Job No. 101 is completed and transferred to the finished goods storeroom. Apply factory overhead to production departments using the predetermined rate calculated in No. 1.

Total direct labor hours are:

Machine department	1,497 hours
Assembly department	1,295 hours

Record factory overhead applied in the general journal. Total all costs and enter data in summary section. Record entry to transfer units to finished goods inventory in the general journal.

January 16, Tuesday
No. 20　　　Sales invoice #002 was issued for Job 101 to Hartley Industries, New York for $59,500. Record sale in sales journal. Marketing and administrative expenses are 5% of sales. Complete the summary section of the job cost sheet. No entry is required for marketing and administrative cost; details are included in the summary data at the end of the month.

January 17, Wednesday
No. 21　　　Received an order from Genis Co., Baltimore, Md., for 250 voltage regulators, the order is due March 30. Job No. 130 was assigned.

No. 22　　　The payroll clerk submits the following report for payment. Record in payroll journal.

Total payroll:
For week ended January 6		$30,157.90
For week ended January 13		32,033.70
		$62,191.60

Deductions:
Employees' federal income tax payable	$9,950.66	
FICA tax payable	4,353.41	14,304.07
Net payroll		$47,887.53

Record the payroll related expenses in the general journal and on the department factory overhead cost sheet as follows:

FICA tax	$ 4,353.41
Federal unemployment tax	497.53
Total payroll related taxes	$ 4,850.94

Machine department	$ 2,244.37
Assembly department	1,394.22
Repairs and maintenance department	663.55
Utilities department	548.80
	$ 4,850.94

January 19, Friday

No. 23 Issued materials to Job No. 130 for $10,920, Req. No. 108.

No. 24 The machine department supervisor reports spoilage (considered in the normal range) on Job No. 108. Salvage value $1,095. Record in general journal and job order cost sheet. Company policy is to charge spoilage to specific jobs; it is not included in the factory overhead application rate.

No. 25 Purchased a new factory machine for $6,000 from Foley Machine Co., Ohio. No entry is required (included in summary at end of month.)

January 22, Monday

No. 26 The following is the payroll report prepared by the payroll clerk for the week ending January 20.

Payroll Summary

Job. No.	Machine Department DL Hours	Machine Department DL Cost	Assembly Department DL Hours	Assembly Department DL Cost	Repairs & Maint. Dept.	Util. Dept.	Total
105	290	$ 1,595.00	141	$ 592.20			$ 2,187.20
108	255	1,402.50	163	684.60			2,087.10
126	285	1,567.50	103	432.60			2,000.10
130	58	319.00	–	–			319.00
Total direct labor		$ 4,884.00		$1,709.40			$ 6,593.40
Indirect labor		2,441.00		2,411.00	$2,601	$2,310	9,763.00
Overtime		510.00		108.00	110	95	823.00
Supervisor's salaries		5,100.00		3,200.00	1,725	900	10,925.00
Total		$12,935.00		$7,428.40	$4,436	$3,305	$28,104.40

No. 27 Job No. 108 is completed and transferred to finished goods storeroom. Apply factory overhead to production departments, total production costs, and record in general journal.

Total direct labor hours as follows:

Machine department	1,774 hours
Assembly department	1,183 hours

No. 28   The machine department reports 8 defective units on Job No. 130. This amount has been determined to be a normal number of defective units for this process. The cost of reworking the defective units is as follows:

Direct materials	$1,120.00
Direct labor	36 machine hours*

Enter material cost on job order cost sheet. Req. No. 109.

Company policy is to charge defective units to specific jobs; it is not included in the factory overhead application rate.

*Labor cost will be included in the payroll summary.

January 24, Wednesday

No. 29   Received an order from Baldwin Electronics, New Jersey; 265 conductor units to be delivered on February 28. Job No. 132 was assigned.

No. 30   Returned to materials storeroom from Job 130 $2,050 of materials. Record in general journal.

January 25, Thursday

No. 31   Issued sales invoice 003 to Tracy Sound Equipment for $67,375 for Job No. 108. Order was picked up by firm.

No. 32   Issued materials to Job No. 132 costing $12,095. Materials Req. No. 110.

No. 33   Issued supplies to Assembly Dept. $890; Req. No. 111.

January 26, Friday

No. 34   Job. No. 126 is completed and the units are transferred to finished goods storeroom until their delivery date.

The following are the direct labor hours in each department for the preceding week:

Machine department	365 hours	$2,007,50
Assembly department	385 hours	$1,617.00

Record on job order cost sheet to bring labor cost up to date.

Total direct labor hours for Job No. 126:

Machine department	949 hours	
Assembly department	624 hours	

Record factory overhead applied; total all costs and enter summary data. Record entry in general journal.

No. 35   Job No. 105 is completed and the units are transferred to finished goods until delivery. The following direct labor hours are for the preceding week:

Machine department	481 hours	$2,645.50
Assembly department	398 hours	$1,671.60

Total direct labor hours for Job 105:

Machine department	2,990 hours
Assembly department	1,795 hours

Enter costs and record in general journal.

January 29, Monday

No. 36   The following payroll report is prepared by the payroll clerk for the week ending January 27.

Payroll Summary

Job. No.	Machine Department DL Hours	Machine Department DL Cost	Assembly Department DL Hours	Assembly Department DL Cost	Repairs & Maint. Dept.	Util. Dept.	Total
126	365	$ 2,007.50	385	$ 1,617.00			$ 3,624.50
105	481	2,645.50	398	1,671.60			4,317.10
130	310*	1,705.00	290	1,218.00			2,923.00
132	140	770.00	33	138.00			908.00
Total direct labor		$ 7,128.00		$ 4,644.60			$11,772.60
Indirect labor		1,965.00		2,365.15	$2,596	$2,365	9,291.15
Overtime		468.50		406.00	211	185	1,270.50
Supervisor's salaries		5,210.00		3,250.00	1,810	950	11,220.00
Total		$14,771.50		$10,665.75	$4,617	$3,500	$33,554.25

*Labor cost includes 36 hours for rework of defective units found in the machine department.

Note:
Jobs 126 and 105 - labor costs were entered on job order cost sheet when jobs were completed.

January 30, Tuesday

No. 37   Issued additional materials to Job 132, Req. No. 112 costing $4,100.

January 31, Wednesday

No. 38   The payroll clerk submits the following report for payment:

Total payroll:

For week ended January 20	$28,104.40
For week ended January 27	33,554.25
	$61,658.65

Deductions:

Employees' federal income tax payable	$9,865.38	
FICA tax payable	4,316.11	14,181.49
Net payroll		$47,477.16

Record the payroll related expenses in the general journal and on the department factory overhead cost sheet as follows:

FICA tax	$ 4,316.11
Federal unemployment tax	493.27
Total payroll related taxes	$ 4,809.38
Machine department	$ 2,161.11
Assembly department	1,411.35
Repairs and maintenance	706.13
Utilities	530.79
	$ 4,809.38

No. 39   Payroll costs incurred since the last payroll summary must be entered on the books to be included in the cost of January operations. Record costs on job cost sheets and in the labor distribution journal. It is not necessary to record deductions, this entry will be reversed at the beginning of next month.

Payroll Summary to January 31

Job. No.	Machine Department DL Hours	Machine Department DL Cost	Assembly Department DL Hours	Assembly Department DL Cost	Repairs & Maint. Dept.	Util. Dept.	Total
130	309	$1,699.50	185	$ 777.00			$ 2,476.50
132	286	1,573.00	118	495.60			2,068.60
Total direct labor		$3,272.50		$1,272.60			$ 4,545.10
Indirect labor		689.00		842.00	$ 612	$ 841	2,984.00
Overtime		91.00		48.00	46	81	266.00
Supervisor's salaries		2,600.00		1,550.00	900	475	5,525.00
Total		$6,652.50		$3,712.60	$1,558	$1,397	$13,320.10

No. 40   The following factory overhead items were incurred during the month. Record entry in the general journal. Post to department factory overhead cost sheets.

	Machine Dept.	Assembly Dept.	Repairs & Maint. Dept.	Util. Dept.	Total
Depreciation- Factory Equipment	$ 330	$ 290	$ 120	$ 85	$ 825
Depreciation- Building	240	210	90	60	600
Expired fire insurance*	320	280	120	80	800
Accrued property taxes	480	420	180	120	1,200
Total	$1,370	$1,200	$ 510	$345	$3,425

*Prepaid expense.

Post transactions in the summary data below to the general ledger accounts:

Account Journal	Number	Account	Debit	Credit
Cash Receipts (CRJ)	101	Cash	200,505.00	
	106	Account receivable		198,905.00
	704	Interest income		1,600.00

Account Journal	Number	Account	Debit	Credit
Cash	201	Accounts payable	31,429.30	
Disbursements	205	Employee's federal		
(CDJ)		income tax payable	27,974.66	
	207	FICA tax payable	23,570.62	
	101	Cash		81,079.58
	705	Cash discount on		
		purchases		1,895.00
Purchase	502	Marketing and admin-		
Journal		strative expenses	14,868.75	
(PURJ)	129	Prepaid expenses	1,200.00	
	642	Interest expense	700.00	
	138	Factory equipment	6,000.00	
	144	Small tools	1,365.00	
	400	Factory overhead control	3,415.00	
	112	Materials	3,100.00	
	201	Accounts payable		30,648.75

Post general journal, sales journal, materials requisition journal, labor distribution journal and payroll journal to the general ledger.

Reconcile the department factory overhead cost sheets (totals) to the factory overhead control account.

Record in the general journal an entry to close factory overhead control and factory overhead applied. Charge Cost of Good Sold with underapplied difference because it is insignificant. Post entry to the general ledger.

Job No.'s 130 and 132 are still in process. Total all columns of the job order cost sheets (pencil footing) to determine the work-in-process inventory. The work-in-process inventory control account should be reconciled with the work-in-process inventory subsidiary ledger.

Take a trial balance of general ledger accounts. Prepare an income statement for the period (ignore earnings per share and income taxes) as well as a schedule of cost of goods sold.

Balance and rule the general ledger accounts.

Kellum Manufacturing Co.
Distribution of Department Costs and
Calculation of Predetermined Factory Overhead Rates

Estimated Costs	Total	Production Departments		Service Departments	
		Machine	Assembly	Repairs and Maintenance	Utilities
Supervisor's Salary	610 000 00	290 000 00	175 000 00	95 000 00	50 000 00
Indirect Labor	535 000 00	150 000 00	125 000 00	130 000 00	130 000 00
Overtime Premium	60 500 00	30 000 00	20 000 00	8 000 00	2 500 00
Supplies	29 500 00	15 000 00	8 000 00	5 000 00	1 500 00
Small Tools	16 200 00	7 000 00	5 000 00	3 100 00	1 100 00
Depreciation-Factory Equipment	10 020 00	4 000 00	3 500 00	1 500 00	1 020 00
Depreciation Building	8 100 00	3 000 00	3 000 00	1 100 00	1 000 00
Fire Insurance	10 000 00	4 000 00	3 500 00	1 500 00	1 000 00
Water	3 100 00				3 100 00
Heat, Light and Power	38 500 00				38 500 00
Property Taxes	14 900 00	6 000 00	5 100 00	2 300 00	1 500 00
Total	1 335 820 00	509 000 00	348 100 00	247 500 00	231 220 00

*Allocation of Service Depts. (refer to next page)

Repairs and Maintenance

Utilities

Total Production Department Overhead

Estimated Direct Labor Hours

Overhead Rate per Direct Labor Hour

17

*Allocate service departments directly to production departments on the following basis:

Repairs and Maintenance - allocate to Utilities, Machine and Assembly Departments per number of service requests.

Utilities - allocate to Production Departments per number of machine hours.

	Total	Machine	Assembly	Repairs and Maintenance	Utilities
Repairs and Maintenance Service Requests	1864	985 (52.8%)	673 (36.1%)		206 (11.1%)
Utilities Machine Hours	137000	94000 (68.6%)	43000 (31.4%)		

Materials Requisition Journal

Date			Req. No.	Work in Process Inventory (Dr) (115)	Factory Overhd. Control (Dr) (400)	Materials (Cr) (112)

Payroll Journal

Date	Payroll Payable (Dr) (203)	Employees' Fed'l Income Tax Payable (Cr) (205)	FICA Tax Payable (Cr) (207)	Cash (Cr) (101)		

20

Labor Distribution Journal

Date	Work-in-Process Inventory (Dr) (115)		Factory Overhead Control (Dr) (400)			Payroll Payable (Cr) (203)
	Machine	Assembly	Indirect Labor	Overtime Premium	Supervisor's Salary	

21

Sales Journal

Date	Account		Sales Number	Accts Rec(Dr106) Sales (Cr)(301)	Cost of Goods Sold (Dr) (351) Finished Goods (Cr) (124)

General Journal

Date	Account	Acct. No.	Debit	Credit

Date	Account	Acct. No.	Debit	Credit

Acct. No.	Account		Debit	Credit
101	Cash		38 1 3 2 00	
103	Notes Receivable		8 5 0 0 00	
106	Accounts Receivable		89 3 5 0 00	
106.1	Allowance for Doubtful Accounts			4 6 0 0 00
112	Materials		62 8 0 0 00	
115	Work in Process Inventory		49 5 4 0 10	
124	Finished Goods Inventory		52 5 0 0 00	
129	Prepaid Expenses		18 0 0 0 00	
130	Land		2 16 0 0 0 00	
133	Building		2 78 0 0 0 00	
133.1	Accumulated Depreciation - Building			83 0 0 0 00
138	Factory Equipment		1 98 0 0 0 00	
138.1	Accumulated Depreciation - Factory Equipment			46 0 0 0 00
144	Small Tools		61 0 0 0 00	
147	Office Equipment		90 0 0 0 00	
201	Accounts Payable			5 49 8 0 10
203	Payroll Payable			5 63 2 5 00
205	Employees' Federal Income Tax Payable			9 2 6 4 20
207	FICA Tax Payable			8 1 0 4 80
210	Federal Unemployment Tax Payable			3 0 1 12
221	Accrued Property Taxes			8 0 0 0 00
250	Capital Stock			3 75 0 0 0 00
262	Retained Earnings			5 16 2 4 6 88
	TOTAL		1 16 1 8 2 2 10	1 16 1 8 2 2 10

General Ledger

	Cash					Acct 101
Date	Item	Posting Reference	Debit	Credit		Balance
Jan 1		√				38132 00

	Notes Receivable					Acct 103
Date	Item	Posting Reference	Debit	Credit		Balance
Jan 1		√				8500 00

	Accounts Receivable					Acct 106
Date	Item	Posting Reference	Debit	Credit		Balance
Jan 1		√				89350 00

	Allowance for Doubtful Accounts					Acct 106.1
Date	Item	Posting Reference	Debit	Credit		Balance
Jan 1		√				4600 00

	Materials				Acct 112
Date	Item	Posting Reference	Debit	Credit	Balance
Jan 1		√			62 800 00

	Work-in-Process Inventory				Acct 115
Date	Item	Posting Reference	Debit	Credit	Balance
Jan 1		√			49 540 10

	Spoiled Units Inventory				Acct 118
Date	Item	Posting Reference	Debit	Credit	Balance

	Finished Goods Inventory				Acct 124
Date	Item	Posting Reference	Debit	Credit	Balance
Jan 1		√			52 500 00

Prepaid Expenses					Acct 129	
Date	Item	Posting Reference	Debit	Credit	Balance	
Jan 1		✓			18 000	00

Land					Acct 130	
Date	Item	Posting Reference	Debit	Credit	Balance	
Jan 1		✓			216 000	00

Building					Acct 133	
Date	Item	Posting Reference	Debit	Credit	Balance	
Jan 1		✓			278 000	00

Accumulated Depreciation – Building					Acct 133.1	
Date	Item	Posting Reference	Debit	Credit	Balance	
Jan 1		✓			83 000	00

Factory Equipment					Acct 138	
Date	Item	Posting Reference	Debit	Credit	Balance	
Jan 1		✓			198 000	00

	Accumulated Depreciation – Factor Equipment				Acct 138.1
Date	Item	Posting Reference	Debit	Credit	Balance
Jan 1		√			4 6 0 0 0 00

	Small Tools				Acct 144
Date	Item	Posting Reference	Debit	Credit	Balance
Jan 1		√			6 1 0 0 0 00

	Office Equipment				Acct 147
Date	Item	Posting Reference	Debit	Credit	Balance
Jan 1		√			9 0 0 0 0 00

	Accounts Payable				Acct 201
Date	Item	Posting Reference	Debit	Credit	Balance
Jan 1		√			5 4 9 8 0 10

	Payroll Payable				Acct 203
Date	Item	Posting Reference	Debit	Credit	Balance
Jan 1		√			5 6 3 2 5 00

General Ledger

	Employees Federal Income Tax Payable				Acct 203
Date	Item	Posting Reference	Debit	Credit	Balance
Jan 1		√			9 2 6 4 20

	FICA Tax Payable				Acct 207
Date	Item	Posting Reference	Debit	Credit	Balance
Jan 1		√			8 1 0 4 80

	Federal Unemployment Tax Payable				Acct 210
Date	Item	Posting Reference	Debit	Credit	Balance
Jan 1		√			3 0 1 12

	Accrued Property Taxes Payable				Acct 221
Date	Item	Posting Reference	Debit	Credit	Balance
Jan 1		√			8 0 0 0 00

	Capital Stock				Acct 250
Date	Item	Posting Reference	Debit	Credit	Balance
Jan 1		√			3 7 5 0 0 0 00

	Retained Earnings				Acct 262	
Date	Item	Posting Reference	Debit	Credit	Balance	
Jan 1		√			5 1 6 24 6 88	

	Sales				Acct 301	
Date	Item	Posting Reference	Debit	Credit	Balance	

	Cost of Goods Sold				Acct 351	
Date	Item	Posting Reference	Debit	Credit	Balance	

	Factory Overhead Applied				Acct 360	
Date	Item	Posting Reference	Debit	Credit	Balance	

	Factory Overhead Control				Acct 400	
Date	Item	Posting Reference	Debit	Credit	Balance	

	Factory Overhead Control	(cont'd)			Acct 400
Date	Item	Posting Reference	Debit	Credit	Balance

	Marketing and Administrative Expenses				Acct 502
Date	Item	Posting Reference	Debit	Credit	Balance

	Interest Expense				Acct 642
Date	Item	Posting Reference	Debit	Credit	Balance

	Interest Income				Acct 704
Date	Item	Posting Reference	Debit	Credit	Balance

	Cash Discount on Purchases				Acct 705
Date	Item	Posting Reference	Debit	Credit	Balance

General Ledger Trial Balance

Acct. No.	Account		Debit	Credit

Kellum Manufacturing Company
Statement of Cost of Goods Sold
For the Month Ended January 31, 19___

		Kellum Manufacturing Company								
		Income Statement								
		For the Period Ending January 31, 19___								

35

Job Order Cost Sheet

Customer: Hartley Industries
Product: Circuit Boards
Quantity: 350

Job Order No.: 101
Date Ordered: Nov. 15, 19___
Date Started: Nov. 22, 19___
Date Requested: Jan. 17, 19___
Date Completed:

Date	Requisition No.	Direct Materials Amount	Direct Labor Departments		Factory Overhead Applied	
			Machine	Assembly	Machine	Assembly
19__						
Jan 1		7600 00	4680 50	3 309 60		

Total

Summary

Selling Price
Factory Costs:
  Direct Materials
  Direct Labor
  Factory Overhead
Gross Profit
Marketing and Administrative
  Expenses
Estimated Profit

36

Job Order Cost Sheet

Customer: Webster Industries
Product: Component Units
Quantity: 600

Job Order No: 105
Date Ordered: Dec. 2, 19___
Date Started: Dec. 6, 19___
Date Requested: Feb. 4, 19___
Date Completed: ___

Date	Requisition No.	Direct Materials Amount	Direct Labor Departments — Machine	Direct Labor Departments — Assembly	Factory Overhead Applied — Machine	Factory Overhead Applied — Assembly
19						
Jan 1		8050 00	8800 00	3150 00		

Total

Summary

Selling Price
Factory Costs:
  Direct Materials
  Direct Labor
  Factory Overhead
Gross Profit
Marketing and Administrative
  Expenses
Estimated Profit

Job Order Cost Sheet

Customer: Tracy Sound Equipment
Product: Amplifying Systems
Quantity: 175

Job Order No.: 108
Date Ordered: Dec. 1, 19___
Date Started: Dec. 8, 19___
Date Requested: Jan. 26, 19___
Date Completed: _____

Date	Requisition No.	Direct Materials Amount	Direct Labor Departments — Machine	Direct Labor Departments — Assembly	Factory Overhead Applied — Machine	Factory Overhead Applied — Assembly
19__						
Jan 1		6 1 9 5 00	4 9 8 0 00	2 7 7 5 00		

Total

Summary
Selling Price
Factory Costs:
  Direct Materials
  Direct Labor
  Factory Overhead
Gross Profit
Marketing and Administrative
  Expenses
Estimated Profit

38

Job Order Cost Sheet

Customer: Sonic Systems
Product: Printed Circuit Boards
Quantity: 500

Job Order No.: 126
Date Ordered: Jan. 5, 19___
Date Started:
Date Requested: March 3, 19___
Date Completed:

Date	Requisition No.	Direct Materials Amount	Direct Labor Departments		Factory Overhead Applied	
			Machine	Assembly	Machine	Assembly

Total

Summary

Selling Price

Factory Costs:
  Direct Materials
  Direct Labor
  Factory Overhead
Gross Profit
Marketing and Administrative
  Expenses
Estimated Profit

39

Job Order Cost Sheet

Customer: Genis Co.
Product: Voltage Regulators
Quantity: 250

Job Order No.: 130
Date Ordered: Jan. 17, 19____
Date Started:
Date Requested: March 30, 19____
Date Completed:

Date	Requisition No.	Direct Materials Amount	Direct Labor Departments		Factory Overhead Applied	
			Machine	Assembly	Machine	Assembly

Total

Summary

Selling Price
Factory Costs:
  Direct Materials
  Direct Labor
  Factory Overhead
Gross Profit
Marketing and Administrative
  Expenses
Estimated Profit

40

Job Order Cost Sheet

Customer: Baldwin Electronics
Product: Conductor Units
Quantity: 265

Job Order No.: 132
Dated Ordered: Jan. 24, 19___
Date Started:
Date Requested: Feb. 28, 19___
Date Completed:

Date	Requisition No.	Direct Materials Amount	Direct Labor Departments		Factory Overhead Applied	
			Machine	Assembly	Machine	Assembly
	Total					
	Summary					
	Selling Price					
	Factory Costs:					
	Direct Materials					
	Direct Labor					
	Factory Overhead					
	Gross Profit					
	Marketing and Administrative					
	Expenses					
	Estimated Profit					

41

Date	Source	Indirect Labor		Overtime Premium		Supervisor's Salary		Payroll Related Taxes		Supplies
	MACHINE DEPT:									
	ASSEMBLY DEPT:									
	REPAIRS & MAINT. DEPT:									
	UTILITIES:									

Factory Overhead Cost Sheet

Small Tools	Depreciation		Fire Insurance	Heat, Light, Power	Water	Property Taxes
	Factory Equipment	Building				

PROCESS COSTING PRACTICE SET

SUNRISER CORPORATION
PRACTICE SET
PROCESS COST ACCOUNTING

PROCESS COSTING

<u>INTRODUCTION</u>

This practice set is designed to illustrate the principles and concepts of a process cost accounting system. The student is the general accountant for a firm which manufactures trumpets. The details concerning purchases of materials, labor operations, and number of completed units as well as other aspects of the accounting system have been condensed to make the case workable, yet comprehensive.

Instructions are given whenever a transaction occurs for the first time. The student will be required to make and post journal entries, and prepare cost of production reports and financial statements.

Upon completion of this practice set, a student will have an understanding of a process cost accounting system and the accumulation of product costs.

The Sunriser Corporation is a manufacturing firm which produces three valve trumpets, through a continuous process. The corporation utilizes four processing departments, three service departments and a selling and administration department.

The following is a brief summary of the manufacturing process that takes place.

Department I is concerned with the shaping of the instrument. Brass tubing is packed with sand and bent to the desired shape. The sand is used to prevent the collapsing of the brass tubing while being bent. Once the desired shape has been obtained, it is transferred to Department II where the joints and other areas are sealed and welded. This is done to eliminate possible air leaks. After this is done, the trumpets are transferred to Department III where the valves are formed and fitted to the trumpets. The valves are made of a special alloy. Finally, the trumpets are transferred to Department IV where the finish (lacquer) is applied to the instruments.

The company utilizes the following records:

1. Voucher register
2. Check register
3. General journal
4. General ledger
5. Cost of production reports

Please note the following:

A.   <u>Department I</u>
FIFO, direct materials, direct labor, factory overhead

        <u>Department II</u>
FIFO, direct labor, factory overhead

        <u>Department III</u>
Weighted average, direct materials*, direct labor, factory overhead

        <u>Department IV</u>
Weighted average, direct materials*, direct labor, factory overhead

        *Direct materials added do <u>not</u> increase units.

        <u>**Factory overhead applied:**</u>

Dept. I	$1.25	times total direct labor dollars of Department I
Dept. II	$ .75	times total direct labor dollars of Department II
Dept. III	$1.00	times total direct labor dollars of Department III
Dept. IV	$ .50	times total direct labor dollars of Department IV

Use factory overhead applied in the cost of productions reports.

B.   You are to use the factory overhead control account for any transaction involving the maintenance department, factory administration department or the shipping and warehousing department.

C.   Materials for all departments are recorded in one materials account.

D.   Any transaction involving a cash disbursement is recorded in the voucher register. Payments are recorded in the check register; no purchased discounts were taken in the month of January.

E.   A subsidiary ledger for the factory overhead control account and the selling and administration expense control account is <u>not</u> required.

F.   Subsidiary records are <u>not</u> required for accounts receivable, materials and finished goods inventory.

Required: Record the following transactions for the month of January:

Transactions for the Month of January

1/2   Paid voucher 144 for $421. Issued check No. 001. Enter in the check register and in the voucher register.

1/2   One ton of high quality brass received from Brass, Inc. for $9,000. Enter in the voucher register as direct materials for Dept. I. Voucher No. 1.

1/2   Two tons of sand used in packing of instruments in Dept. I, were delivered for $120 by The Sand Co. Considered a factory overhead item. Voucher No. 2.

1/3   One ton of a special alloy used in Dept. III was delivered by Acme Steel Co. for $8,000. Considered direct materials for Dept. III. Voucher No. 3.

1/3   A new typewriter for the factory office was purchased on credit from Typewriters of America for $150. Voucher No. 4. Considered a factory overhead item.

1/4   Paid voucher No. 143 for $500. Issued check No. 002.

1/5   Freight bill of $500 received from R.S. Trucking Co. Voucher No. 5. Considered a factory overhead item.

1/5   Repair parts costing $250 were purchased on credit from Machinery, Inc. Considered a factory overhead item. Voucher No. 6.

1/6   Heating oil for the month costing $20,050 was delivered by Son & Son Oil Co. Considered a factory overhead item. Voucher No. 7.

1/6   Paid voucher No. 145 for $450. Issued check No. 003.

Factory Payroll

1/6

Department	Gross Pay
Processing departments:	
I	$ 9,250
II	2,120
III	10,125
IV	1,175
Factory overhead:	
Maintenance	855
Factory administration	1,055
Shipping and warehousing	1,250
Total	$25,830

Federal income tax withheld was $3,874.50; FICA withheld was $1,808.10. Voucher No. 8, check No. 004 was for net payroll. Debit payroll payable for gross pay of $25,830. The payroll will be distributed at the end of the month to the various departments.

1/9   Maintenance supplies totaling $5,570 were purchased on credit form O'Henry's Supply Co. Voucher No. 9.

1/9   Paid voucher No. 1, issuing check No. 005.

1/10   Received two tons of high quality brass from Brass, Inc. for $18,000. Voucher No. 10.

1/11   Lacquer materials in solid form totaling $5,000 were received from Finishes, Inc. Direct materials are used in Dept. IV. Voucher No. 11.

1/12   Paid voucher No. 2 for $120. Issued check No. 006.

1/12   Stationary and other supplies for the factory administration department totaling $850 was purchased on credit from the Office Supply Co. Considered a factory overhead item. Voucher No. 12.

1/12   Invoice for warehousing totaling $1,025 received from Brother's Warehousing Co. Voucher No. 13.

Factory Payroll

1/13

Department	Gross Pay
Processing departments:	
I	$10,525
II	3,755
III	8,575
IV	1,990
Factory overhead:	
Maintenance	900
Factory administration	850
Shipping and warehousing	1,300
Total	$27,895

Federal income tax withheld was $4,184.25; FICA withheld was $1,952.65. Voucher No. 14, check No. 007.

1/13   Biweekly payroll of selling and administration department was:

Gross pay	$12,260.00
Federal income tax withheld	$ 1,839.00
FICA withheld	$ 858.20

Voucher No. 15, check No. 008.

1/13	Paid voucher No. 3, issuing check No. 009.

1/16	Issued check No. 010 for payment of state unemployment tax of $6,145. Voucher No. 16, payable to State Dept. of Revenue and Finance.

1/17	Health insurance premiums totaling $15,195 were paid. Considered a factory overhead item. Voucher No. 17, check No. 011. Voucher payable to Health and Life Insurance Co.

1/17	Paid voucher No. 4 for $150 issuing check No. 012. Paid freight bill of $500. Voucher No. 5, issuing check No. 013.

1/18	Received one ton of high quality brass form Brass, Inc. for $9,000. Voucher No. 18.

1/18	Paid voucher No. 6 for $250. Issued check No. 014.

1/19	Replacement parts for the maintenance department totaling $500 were purchased from L & M Supply Co. Voucher No. 19, check No. 015.

1/19	Lacquer materials totaling $2,750 were received from Finishes, Inc. Voucher No. 20.

Factory Payroll

1/20

Department	Gross Pay
Processing departments:	
I	$10,450
II	3,200
III	8,845
IV	2,150
Factory overhead:	
Maintenance	1,055
Factory administration	990
Shipping and warehousing	1,345
Total	$28,035

Federal income tax withheld was $4,205.25; FICA withheld was $1,962.45. Voucher No. 21, check No. 016.

1/20	Forwarded federal income tax withheld of $18,577.89. Voucher No. 22 payable to Internal Revenue Service. Check No. 017.

1/20	Issued check No. 018 for employee and employer FICA payable of $17,211.62. Voucher No. 23 payable to Internal Revenue Service. (Charge $8,605.81 to each payable account.)

51

1/23	Paid voucher No. 9; issuing check No. 019. Paid voucher No. 10; issuing check No. 020. Paid voucher No. 12; issuing check No. 021 for $850.
1/24	Received one ton of a special alloy, delivered by Acme Steel Co. for $8,000. Direct materials for Dept. III. Voucher No. 24.
1/24	Paid voucher No. 7; issuing check No. 022.
1/25	Declaration of a dividend of 50 cents/share of common stock outstanding. The dividend is payable February 22 to stockholders of record February 8. 40,000 shares are outstanding. Record in general journal. (Upon payment in February entry will be made to voucher register.)
1/25	Maintenance supplies were purchased for $1,050 from Keil's Supply Co. Voucher No. 25, check No. 023.
1/25	Paid voucher No. 11; issuing check No. 024.
1/26	Received welding materials used in Dept. II for $500. The materials are considered a factory overhead item. Voucher No. 26 payable to Welding Unlimited.
1/26	Paid voucher No. 13; issuing check No. 025 for $1,025.
1/26	Received packaging material from U. S. Manufacturing Supply Co. totaling $5,025. Considered a factory overhead item. Voucher No. 27.

Factory Payroll

1/27	Department	Gross Pay
	Processing departments:	
	I	$ 8,775
	II	1,425
	III	6,410
	IV	2,860
	Factory overhead:	
	Maintenance	1,225
	Factory administration	1,175
	Shipping and warehousing	1,430
	Total	$23,300

Federal income tax withheld was $3,495; FICA withheld was $1,631.00. Voucher No. 28, check No. 026.

1/27	Biweekly payroll of selling and administration department was:

Gross pay	$10,020.00
Federal income tax withheld	$ 1,503.00
FICA withheld	$ 701.40
Voucher No. 29, check No. 027.	

1/27   Paid voucher No. 18; issuing check No. 028.

1/30   Paid voucher No. 20; issuing check No. 029 for $2,750.

1/31   Received electric bill for factory from U. S. Power for $4,025. Voucher No. 30.

1/31   Received January's water bill of $1,500 from Water District 384. Voucher No. 31.

1/31   Selling and administration expenses vouchered and paid $45,350. Voucher No. 32, check No. 030. Debit selling and administration expense control account in the voucher register.

1/31   Paid $5,325 for advanced courses for employees. Considered a factory overhead item, voucher 33 payable to Trade & Technical School. Issued check No. 031.

Summation of Monthly Activities

No. 1

Accrued Payroll - 2 days

Department	Gross Pay
Processing departments:	
I	$ 1,000
II	500
III	1,045
IV	525
Factory overhead:	
Maintenance	400
Factory administration	300
Shipping and warehousing	500
Total factory accrued payroll	$ 4,270
Selling and administration department accrued payroll	$ 2,025

Make an entry in the general journal to distribute to the various departments total payroll (actual and accrued) for the month.

No. 2   Employer's payroll taxes are as follows:

	Total	FICA	Federal Unemploy. Tax	State Unemploy. Tax
To Factory Overhead Control	$ 9,875.64	$7,354.20	$ 840.48	$1,680.96
To Selling and Admin. Expense Control	2,094.32	1,559.60	178.24	356.48
Total	$11,969.96	$8,913.80	$1,018.72	$2,037.44

Make the journal entry to distribute the employer's payroll taxes.

No. 3   Fire insurance premiums totaling $3,100 expired; $450 represents selling and administration expense. Make the necessary journal entry.

No. 4   Property taxes for January totaling $4,000 are to be accrued. Of this amount $700 represents selling & administration expense. Make the necessary journal entry.

No. 5   Sales for the month were $549,000. Make the necessary journal entry. Debit accounts receivable.

No. 6   Cash receipts for the month were $400,000. Make the required journal entry. Credit accounts receivable.

No. 7   Accrue interest on notes payable and bonds payable, $250 and $3,000, respectively. Record in journal. Considered a selling and administration expense.

No. 8   Depreciation is as follows for the month of January:

Factory overhead:
　　Building $ 700
　　Machinery $4,000
Selling and administration:
　　Office furniture and fixtures $ 650

No. 9   Bad debt expense is estimated to be $3,000 for the month of January. Bad debt expense is considered a selling and administration expense. Make the required entry.

Developing the Cost of Production Reports
For Departments I, II, II, and IV

No. 10

Departments I and II
Both Departments Use FIFO

Units:	Dept. I	Dept. II

Beginning units in process:
    Dept. I
    100% direct materials,
    40% conversion costs
    Dept. II
    100% direct materials,
    30% conversion costs
	600	450

Started in process during period	3,000	
Units received from Dept. I		2,500
Transferred to Dept. III		2,600

Ending units in process:
    Dept. I
    100% direct materials,
    50% conversion costs
    Dept. II
    100% direct materials,
    60% conversion costs
	1,100	350

Costs:

	Dept. I	Dept. II
Beginning work-in-process inventory:		
From Dept. I		$3,000
Direct materials	$10,000	-0-
Direct labor	15,000	2,500
Factory overhead (applied)	18,750	1,875
Total	$43,750	$7,375
Added during period:		
Direct materials	$25,000	-0-
Direct labor	Determine from entries	Determine from entries
Factory overhead (applied; rate x labor dollars)	$1.25 x total direct labor dollars	$.75 x total direct labor dollars
Total	$115,000	$ 19,250

Complete the above information for Departments I and II.
Complete the cost of production reports for both departments.
Make the journal entries for direct materials used, factory
overhead applied, and units transferred. Don't forget that
the Departments use FIFO.

No. 11

Departments III and IV

Both Departments Use Weighted Average

Units:	Dept. III	Dept. IV
Beginning units in process:	700	70
Dept. III		
100% direct materials,		
20% conversion costs		
Dept. IV		
100% direct materials,		
50% conversion costs		
Units from Dept. II	2,600	
Units from Dept. III		3,050
Transferred to finished goods		2,900
Ending units in process:	250	220
Dept. III		
100% direct materials		
60% conversion costs		
Dept. IV		
50% direct materials,		
50% conversion costs		

Costs:	Dept. III	Dept. IV
Beginning work-in-process inventory:		
From preceding department	$50,000	$6,300
Direct materials	3,000	150
Direct labor	3,000	200
Factory overhead (applied)	3,000	100
Total	$59,000	$6,750

Added during period:		
Direct materials	$15,000	$6,500
Direct labor	Determine from entries	Determine from entries
Factory overhead (applied; rate x labor dollars)	$1 x total direct labor dollars	$.50 x total direct labor dollars
Total	$85,000	$19,550

Complete the above information for Departments III and IV. Complete the cost of production reports for both departments. Make the journal entries for direct materials used, factory overhead applied and units transferred. Don't forget the departments use weighted average.

No. 12   The cost of goods sold is determined from the finished goods inventory which is dept on a FIFO basis. Records show finished goods beginning inventory of 750 units priced at $91. Units sold in January totaled 3,050 units. Determine the cost of goods sold and make the required entry. Show computations.

No. 13   Rule and balance the check register and voucher register. Post to the general ledger. Post all entries in the general journal to the general ledger.

No. 14   Factory overhead for the month of January:

overapplied	$ 809.36
applied factory overhead	$97,600.00
actual factory overhead	$96,790.64

Make a closing entry for the two accounts and credit the difference to cost of goods sold.

No. 15   Prepare a general ledger trial balance for the month of January.

No. 16   Prepare a cost of goods manufactured statement and a schedule of cost of goods sold for the month of January.

No. 17   Assume the following two ledger accounts in addition to those already stated. Income tax expense - debit balance January 31 of $75,066.64. Income tax payable - credit balance January 31 of $75,066.64. Record in the general journal and post to the general ledger.

Prepare an income statement for the month of January (ignore earnings per share). Use the selling and administration expense control account to account for depreciation, interest, payroll taxes, etc.

No. 18   Record closing entries in the general journal. Make sure you close the income tax expense account. Utilize an income summary account. Post to general ledger. Rule the general ledger.

No. 19   Prepare a classified balance sheet as of January 31, 19XX.

Check Register

Date	Ck. No.	Payee	Voucher No.	Vouchers Payable (Dr) (200)	Purchases Discount (Cr) (610)	Cash (Cr) (100)

58

Date	Account	Ref.	Debit	Credit

General Journal

Date	Account	Ref.	Debit	Credit

General Journal

Date	Account	Ref.	Debit	Credit

	Cash					Acct. 100	
Date	Item	Posting	Reference	Debit	Credit	Balance (Dr)	
Jan 1		√				5 0 0 5 0	--

	Accounts Receivable					Acct. 105	
Date	Item	Posting	Reference	Debit	Credit	Balance (Dr)	
Jan 1		√				3 0 0 5 5 0	--

	Allowance for Doubtful Accounts					Acct. 106	
Date	Item	Posting	Reference	Debit	Credit	Balance (Cr)	
Jan 1		√				6 1 2 5	--

	Unexpired Fire Insurance					Acct. 110	
Date	Item	Posting	Reference	Debit	Credit	Balance (Dr)	
Jan 1		√				3 7 2 0 0	--

	Materials					Acct. 115	
Date	Item	Posting	Reference	Debit	Credit	Balance (Dr)	
Jan 1		√				5 0 0 0 0	--

	Work-in-Process Inventory-Dept I					Acct. 120	
Date	Item	Posting	Reference	Debit	Credit	Balance (Dr)	
Jan 1		√				4 3 7 5 0	--

	Work-in-Process Inventory-Dept II				Acct. 125
Date	Item	Posting Reference	Debit	Credit	Balance (Dr)
Jan 1		√			7375--

	Work-in-Process Inventory-Dept III				Acct. 130
Date	Item	Posting Reference	Debit	Credit	Balance (Dr)
Jan 1		√			59000--

	Work-in-Process Inventory-Dept IV				Acct. 135
Date	Item	Posting Reference	Debit	Credit	Balance (Dr)
Jan 1		√			6750--

	Finished Goods Inventory				Acct. 140
Date	Item	Posting Reference	Debit	Credit	Balance (Dr)
Jan 1		√			75750--

	Land				Acct. 145
Date	Item	Posting Reference	Debit	Credit	Balance (Dr)
Jan 1		√			525000--

	Building				Acct. 150
Date	Item	Posting Reference	Debit	Credit	Balance (Dr)
Jan 1		√			327500--

	Accumulated Depreciation- Building				Acct. 151
Date	Item	Posting Reference	Debit	Credit	Balance (Cr)
Jan 1		√			81875--

	Machinery								Acct. 155	
Date	Item	Posting Reference		Debit		Credit			Balance (Dr)	
Jan 1		✓							9 5 0 5 7 5	--

	Accumulated Depreciation- Machinery								Acct. 156	
Date	Item	Posting Reference		Debit		Credit			Balance (Cr)	
Jan 1		✓							3 3 7 6 5 0	--

	Office Furniture & Fixtures								Acct. 160	
Date	Item	Posting Reference		Debit		Credit			Balance (Dr)	
Jan 1		✓							7 5 7 5 0	--

	Accumulated Depreciation- Office Furniture & Fixtures								Acct. 161	
Date	Item	Posting Reference		Debit		Credit			Balance (Cr)	
Jan 1		✓							3 0 2 5 0	

	Vouchers Payable								Acct. 200	
Date	Item	Posting Reference		Debit		Credit			Balance (Cr)	
Jan 1		✓							1 3 7 1	--

	Payroll Payable								Acct. 205	
Date	Item	Posting Reference		Debit		Credit			Balance (Cr)	

	Federal Income Tax Withheld								Acct. 210	
Date	Item	Posting Reference		Debit		Credit			Balance (Cr)	
Jan 1		✓							8 6 8 0 14	

	Employee FICA Tax Payable					Acct. 215
Date	Item	Posting Reference	Debit		Credit	Balance (Cr)
Jan 1		√				3 9 8 6 86

	Employer FICA Tax Payable					Acct. 220
Date	Item	Posting Reference	Debit		Credit	Balance (Cr)
Jan 1		√				3 9 8 6 86

	Federal Unemployment Tax Payable					Acct. 225
Date	Item	Posting Reference	Debit		Credit	Balance (Cr)
Jan 1		√				5 4 5 50

	State Unemployment Tax Payable					Acct. 230
Date	Item	Posting Reference	Debit		Credit	Balance (Cr)
Jan 1		√				6 1 4 5 --

	Property Tax Payable					Acct. 235
Date	Item	Posting Reference	Debit		Credit	Balance (Cr)

	Notes Payable					Acct. 240
Date	Item	Posting Reference	Debit		Credit	Balance (Cr)
Jan 1		√				3 00 0 0 --

	Dividends Payable					Acct. 245
Date	Item	Posting Reference	Debit		Credit	Balance (Cr)

	Interest Payable					Acct. 250
Date	Item	Posting Reference	Debit		Credit	Balance (Cr)

Income Tax Payable					Acct. 255
Date	Item	Posting Reference	Debit	Credit	Balance

Bonds Payable					Acct. 260
Date	Item	Posting Reference	Debit	Credit	Balance (Cr)
Jan 1		√			400000 --

Common Stock					Acct. 300
Date	Item	Posting Reference	Debit	Credit	Balance (Cr)
Jan 1		√			1000000 --

Retained Earnings					Acct. 330
Date	Item	Posting Reference	Debit	Credit	Balance (Cr)
Jan 1		√			598634 64

Dividends					Acct. 335
Date	Item	Posting Reference	Debit	Credit	Balance (Dr)

Income Summary					Acct. 400
Date	Item	Posting Reference	Debit	Credit	Balance

Sales					Acct. 500
Date	Item	Posting Reference	Debit	Credit	Balance (Cr)

Factory Overhead-Control					Acct. 600
Date	Item	Posting Reference	Debit	Credit	Balance (Dr)

	Factory Overhead-Applied				Acct. 605
Date	Item	Posting Reference	Debit	Credit	Balance (Cr)

	Purchase Discount				Acct. 610
Date	Item	Posting Reference	Debit	Credit	Balance (Cr)

	Cost of Goods Sold				Acct. 615
Date	Item	Posting Reference	Debit	Credit	Balance (Dr)

	Selling & Administration Expense Control				Acct. 620
Date	Item	Posting Reference	Debit	Credit	Balance (Dr)

	Income Tax Expense				Acct. 625
Date	Item	Posting Reference	Debit	Credit	Balance

Acct. No.		Account		Debit	Credit

| | | Cost of Production Report | | | |
| | | Department I - FIFO | | | |

		Cost of Production Report			
		Department II - FIFO			

| | | Cost of Production Report | | | |
| | | Department II - FIFO (cont'd.) | | | |

Cost of Production Report
Department III - Weighted Average

| | | Cost of Production Report | | | | |
| | | Department IV - Weighted Average | | | | |

Sunriser Corporation

Cost of Goods Manufactured Statement

For the Month Ended January 31, 19__

Sunriser Corporation
Schedule of Cost of Goods Sold
For the Month Ended January 31, 19___

Sunriser Corporation

Income Statement

For the Month Ended January 31, 19___

Sunriser Corporation
Balance Sheet
January 31, 19___

Date	Voucher No.	Payee	Paid Date	Check No.	Vouchers Payable (Cr) (200)	Materials (Dr) (115)	Payroll Payable (Dr) (205)	Federal Tax Wi (Dr) (210)
12/27	143	Office Supply Co.			50000			
12/28	144	E.F. Storage Co.			42100			
12/29	145	Machinery Inc.			45000			
					137100			

Income thheld (Cr) (210)	Employee's Tax (Dr) (215)	FICA Payable (Cr) (215)	Employer FICA Tax Payable (Dr) (220)	State Unempl. Tax Payable (Dr) (230)	Factory Overhd Control (Dr) (600)	Selling and Admn.Exp. (Dr) (620)